This study guide is designed to be used with *Beginning How to Explain and Defend the Catholic Faith* by Father Frank Chacon and Jim Burnham. We have arranged the material into twelve units, suitable for weekly or monthly meetings. Each unit takes approximately 45 minutes.

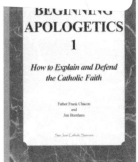

MEETING DATE: TOPIC:

(FILL IN)

UNIT 1 _____ THE EUCHARIST (PP. 7–9 IN *BEGINNING APOLOGETICS 1*)

UNIT 2 _____ THE CANON OF THE BIBLE (PP. 10–12)

UNIT 3 _____ THE BIBLE ALONE? (P. 13)

UNIT 4 _____ APOSTOLIC AUTHORITY: PETER & THE PAPACY (PP. 14–17)

UNIT 5 _____ MARIAN DOCTRINES (PP. 18–20)

UNIT 6 _____ QUESTIONS ASKED ABOUT MARY (PP. 21–23)

UNIT 7 _____ CONFESSION & SCANDALS IN THE CHURCH (PP. 24–26)

UNIT 8 _____ PRAYER TO THE SAINTS (PP. 27–29)

UNIT 9 _____ PURGATORY (PP. 30–33)

UNIT 10 _____ MISCELLANEOUS QUESTIONS 1–5: CALLING PRIESTS "FATHER", STATUES, PAGANISM, SACRIFICE OF THE MASS, BAPTISMAL REGENERATION (PP. 34–36)

UNIT 11 _____ MISCELLANEOUS QUESTIONS 6–9: INFANT BAPTISM, FAITH ALONE, GOOD WORKS, ASSURANCE OF SALVATION (PP. 36–37)

UNIT 12 _____ MISCELLANEOUS QUESTIONS 10–14: TRADITION, DOCTRINAL DEVELOPMENT, PRIESTLY CELIBACY, DIFFERENT DENOMINATIONS, CHRIST'S ONE TRUE CHURCH (PP. 38–39)

Good news! BA1 has 8 more pages. **Not so good news:** You'll have to adjust BA1 page references. But we trust it will be worth the extra effort.

HOW TO USE THIS STUDY GUIDE

This study guide is suitable for individuals, small groups, families, or religious classes. Here is one possible format for using this study guide in a small group (feel free to adapt it to your own needs):

① THE PREPARATION

- Read the assigned pages in *Beginning Apologetics 1* **before** each meeting.
- Sometime before the first meeting, read the introductory material on pages 4–6 of *Beginning Apologetics 1*. This covers practical dos and don'ts for apologetics and Bible reading. Pay particular attention to points 2 and 12 of the first section that stress the importance of charity and patience.

② THE PROGRAM

- begin with prayer
- introduce the topic briefly
- read and discuss the study questions
- end with prayer

③ THE TEAMS

Divide your group into three teams:

- scripture team
- catechism team
- early Church Fathers team

Each team is responsible for looking up beforehand all the references from the Bible, catechism, or early Church Fathers and reading them to the group at the appropriate question.

④ THE TOOLS

All the tools listed are available through San Juan Catholic Seminars (877.327.5343) or the Family Life Center (800.705.6131). An order form is available on the inside cover or you can go on-line at *www.CatholicApologetics.com*. Quantity discounts available through SJCS:

- This **study guide** (Item #SG–BA1).
- ***Beginning Apologetics 1: How to Explain and Defend the Catholic Faith*** (Item #BA–1). Quantity discounts available through SJCS.

- A good **Catholic Bible**. We recommend the *Revised Standard Version-Catholic Edition* (RSVCE, Item #IHP–91X) or the *New American Bible* (NAB). Bible verses are cited book, chapter, and verse. For example, **Matthew 16:18** refers to the book of Matthew, chapter 16, verse 18:

    > And I tell you, you are Peter, and on this rock I will build my church, and the powers of death shall not prevail against it.

- *Catechism of the Catholic Church* (Item #CCC–108). Passages from the *Catechism of the Catholic Church* are abbreviated "*CCC*," followed by the section number. For example, *CCC* **1996** refers to section number 1996:

    > Our justification comes from the grace of God. Grace is favor, the *free and undeserved help* that God gives us to respond to his call to become children of God, adoptive sons, partakers of the divine nature and of eternal life.

- *The Faith of the Early Fathers*, edited by William A. Jurgens (Item #FEF–250). This three-volume set contains the writings of the early Church Fathers. Although all three volumes are valuable, only volume one is necessary for your group. Passages from *The Faith of the Early Fathers* are abbreviated "Jurgens," followed by the section number. For example, **Jurgens 65** refers to section number 65 on page 25, from St. Ignatius' letter to the Smyrnaeans:

    > You must all follow the bishop as Jesus Christ follows the Father, and the presbytery as you would the Apostles. Reverence the deacons as you would the command of God. Let no one do anything of concern to the Church without the bishop. Let that be considered a valid Eucharist which is celebrated by the bishop, or by one whom he appoints. Wherever the bishop appears, let the people be there; just as wherever Jesus Christ is, there is the Catholic Church.

    Jurgens has a wonderful doctrinal index at the back that allows you to quickly discover what the early Fathers believed about dozens of doctrines. Check out Steve Wood's excellent audio tape "How to Use Jurgens."

Each person should have his own copy of this study guide and *Beginning Apologetics 1*. Ideally, each person would also have his own copy of the Bible, the new Catechism, and Jurgens. But it is sufficient if at least one person in each team has the appropriate resource.

These resources, along with those recommended in the **Digging Deeper** sections, are available from:

San Juan Catholic Seminars
P. O. Box 5253 • Farmington, NM 87499
phone: 877.327.5343 • fax: 505.327.5343
e-mail: Begin@CatholicApologetics.com • website: www.CatholicApologetics.com

(Read pages 7–9)

Discussion Questions:

1. Do you believe God really can do things that are totally beyond human comprehension, such as create the world out of nothing (John 1:3) or become a man (John 1:14)? What are some other beliefs that we accept in faith even though we cannot fully comprehend them?

2. Have someone read John 6:51–58 out loud. Imagine you are hearing this for the first time. How would the average person interpret Jesus' words?

3. Do the Jews find Jesus' teaching hard to accept? (See John 6:52.) Do any of Jesus' disciples find the Eucharist hard to accept? (See John 6:60, 66.) How do Peter and the faithful Apostles respond to this difficult teaching? (See John 6:67–68.)

4. Do the Jews, the disciples, and the Apostles interpret Jesus as speaking symbolically or literally about eating his flesh and blood?

5. If a picture is worth a thousand words, then surely a live presentation is worth a thousand pictures. The Jews, the disciples, and the Apostles all heard Jesus "live" and in person. If they all testify that Jesus was speaking literally, is it reasonable for anyone—reading a translation of ancient languages nearly 2000 years later—to maintain that Jesus was speaking only symbolically?

6. Is it inconsistent for Fundamentalists to claim to read the Bible literally when they interpret John 6 symbolically?

7. Is the Eucharist a greater miracle than the manna in the desert? (See John 6:49–51.) Is the Eucharist a greater miracle than the feeding of the 5000? (See John 6:23–27.) Can the Eucharist be greater than these two miracles if it is only symbolic, earthly bread?

8. How does St. Paul understand the Eucharist? Read 1 Corinthians 10:16 and 11:27–29. Does this sound like the language of symbolism?

9. How did the earliest Christians understand the Eucharist? St. Ignatius of Antioch was a disciple and a co-worker of the Apostle John. He was martyred as an old man in Rome around 110 AD, about 10 years after the death of St. John. Who could be a better interpreter of John 6 than an intimate disciple of the author? Listen how St. Ignatius condemns those who deny the Real Presence of Christ in the Eucharist:

    > Take note of those who hold heterodox opinions on the grace of Jesus Christ which has come to us, and see how contrary their opinions are to the mind of God…. They abstain from the Eucharist and from prayer, because **they do not confess that the Eucharist is the Flesh of our Savior Jesus Christ**, Flesh which suffered for our sins and which the Father, in His goodness raised up again. They who deny the gift of God are perishing in their disputes. (*Letter to the Smyrnaeans* 6, 2; Jurgens 64).

10. Read *CCC* 1374–1378 for a beautiful summary of this crown jewel of our faith. Ask yourself:
    - Do I believe that Jesus is really and truly present in the Eucharist? What can I do to strengthen my faith in the Real Presence?
    - Do I receive the Eucharist frequently (*CCC* 1417) and in a state of grace (*CCC* 1416)?
    - How can I demonstrate my belief in the Real Presence? What can I do to strengthen my children's belief in the Real Presence?

Digging Deeper:
CCC 1322–1419.
Jurgens 54a, 64, 128, 249, 846, 848, 870.
Chacon & Burnham, *Beginning Apologetics 3: How to Explain & Defend the Real Presence of Christ in the Eucharist* (San Juan Catholic Seminars, 1999). Item #BA–3.
Mark P. Shea, *This is My Body: An Evangelical Discovers the Real Presence* (Christendom Press, 1993).

(Read pages 10–12)

Discussion Questions:

1. Is the Bible's table of contents part of the inspired text? Did the Bible fall from heaven preprinted and bound in a single volume? Does the Bible anywhere tell us which books belong in it?

2. How do we know which books are inspired and authoritative (and thus deserve to be included in the canon of the Bible)? Why is this an important question?

3. Luther held that a book belonged in the canon if it taught salvation by faith alone. Calvin said that the only way to know a book is inspired is by the internal witness of the Holy Spirit. Using standards like Luther's and Calvin's, what would prevent someone from rejecting huge portions of the Bible and rewriting the canon any way he liked?

4. Did the Old Testament Bible (Septuagint) used by the Apostolic Church have 39 or 46 books?

5. Did the Old Testament canonized by the 4th-century Church have 39 or 46 books?

6. Did Catholics add seven books to the Bible in the 1500s, or did Luther take seven books away?

7. Is there any disagreement among Christians about the 27 books that make up the NT?

8. Whom should Christians thank for gathering, preserving, and establishing the Scriptures? (If you say the Holy Spirit, then what vehicle did the Holy Spirit use to accomplish these things?)

9. Is it reasonable for Christians to trust the authority of the Catholic Church when it comes to determining the contents of the Bible, then reject her authority when it comes to interpreting the Bible?

10. Does the Catholic Church forbid or encourage reading the Bible? (See *CCC* 133.)

11. The following questions can be answered from Henry Graham's *Where We Got the Bible*:

    - Why did the Catholic Church chain Bibles in churches? (Hint: why are phone books chained at public phones or pens chained at banks? See pp. 85–86.)
    - Why did the Catholic Church keep the Bible in Latin for so many years? (Hint: what language did everyone who could read and write use? See pp. 89–91.)
    - Why did the Catholic Church burn certain Bibles? (Hint: what do you do with a misprinted letter? See pp. 129–132.)
    - Why did the Catholic Church sometimes prohibit reading certain versions of the Bible? (See pp. 110–112, 116–121.)

Digging Deeper:
CCC 105, 119, 120, 138.
Jurgens 910t.
Mark P. Shea, *By What Authority: An Evangelical Discovers Catholic Tradition* (Our Sunday Visitor, 1996). Item #BWA–510.
Henry G. Graham, *Where We Got the Bible: Our Debt to the Catholic Church* (TAN Books, 1977). Item #WWGB–042.

(Read page 13)

Discussion Questions:

1. If, as *sola scriptura* claims, all Christian beliefs must come from the Bible, then shouldn't that fundamental belief itself be found in the Bible? Is there a single verse in the Bible that teaches *sola scriptura*?

2. Does 2 Timothy 3:16 really teach *sola scriptura* as many Protestants claim? (Hints: "all scripture" should not be forced into meaning "only scripture." Also, the previous verse, 2 Timothy 3:15, shows that St. Paul is describing the Old Testament scriptures; there wasn't a New Testament in existence when Timothy was a child. No Christian is arguing for *Sola Old Testament*!)

3. Many Protestants claim that 2 Timothy 3:17 implies *sola scriptura* because Scripture makes a Christian "complete, equipped for every good work." Is Scripture the ONLY thing that makes a Christian complete or fully equipped? Look up James 1:4, which says perseverance makes us "perfect and complete, lacking in nothing"; see also 2 Timothy 2:19–21. If 2 Timothy 3:17 proves *sola scriptura*, then wouldn't James 1:4 prove *sola perseverance*? Does this approach lead to conclusions that even Protestants wouldn't accept?

4. If *sola scriptura* can't be found in the scriptures, then doesn't this belief contradict itself?

5. Do any verses in the Bible provide an authoritative list of what books should be included in scripture? If one were to adhere strictly to *sola scriptura*, shouldn't such a list be found in the Bible?

6. Isn't the authoritative list of inspired books an essential religious truth that is found outside the Bible? Doesn't this disprove *sola scriptura*?

7. Does the word "tradition" always have a negative connotation in scripture? (See Matthew 15:2–6; Mark 7:3–7; Colossians 2:8; contrast previous verses with 2 Thessalonians 2:15, 3:6; 1 Corinthians 11:2.)

8. If you ask a Protestant friend, "What is the pillar and foundation of the truth?" what are they likely to give as an answer? What does the Bible give as the answer? (See 1 Timothy 3:15.)

9. What does the *Catechism of the Catholic Church* say about the need for both Sacred Scripture and Sacred Tradition? (See *CCC* 80–82.)

10. What do the early Church Fathers say about the need for both Sacred Scripture and Sacred Tradition? (See Jurgens 213, 242, 291, 443.)

11. What are the tragic results of everyone thinking he can accurately interpret the Bible without the aid of Sacred Tradition?

12. Why would Catholics want to use a good study Bible, like the *Navarre Bible* series, which includes comments from the popes, Church encyclicals, fathers, and councils? (See *CCC* 84–87.)

Digging Deeper:
Steve Wood, "Sola Scriptura? Is the Bible the Sole Rule of Faith?" (audiotape with study guide).
Mark P. Shea, *By What Authority: An Evangelical Discovers Catholic Tradition* (Our Sunday Visitor, 1996). Item #BWA–510.

Unit 4   Apostolic Authority: Peter and the Papacy

(Read pages 14–17)

Discussion Questions:

1. At Cesarea Phillipi (Matthew 16:13), there is a massive rock plateau approximately 200 feet high by 500 feet long. What does this geographical background suggest about the stability of the Church Jesus founded on Peter?

2. What will happen to any church that isn't founded upon a rock? Read Matthew 7:24–27. (Remember, 1 Timothy 3:15 describes the Church as "the household of God.")

3. Some Protestants make a big deal about the two different Greek words used in Matthew 16:18 (see footnote 18 on page 14 of *Beginning Apologetics 1*). Was Jesus speaking Greek or Aramaic at this scene? (Look up the following verses where Peter is called by the Aramaic name "Kephas": John 1:42; 1 Corinthians 1:12, 3:22, 9:5, 15:5; Galatians 1:18, 2:9, 11, 14. Do these nine verses reassure us that Jesus was speaking Aramaic in Matthew 16:18?)

4. In the Aramaic, is there a difference between the words used for "Peter" and "rock"?

5. Compare the authority given to Peter (Matthew 16:13–18) with the authority given to the other Apostles (Matthew 18:18). What is Peter given that the others are not?

6. Look up the following passages where Peter is singled out in Scripture:
   - Luke 22:31–32—Jesus prays for Peter's faith; Peter will then strengthen the other disciples.
   - John 21:15–17—in a threefold commission, Jesus appoints Peter as shepherd of the Church.
   - Acts 15:7–12—after much debate about circumcision, Peter's remarks silenced the whole assembly; the first Church council adopted his decision.

   If we deny a unique role to St. Peter, are we being faithful to the teachings of the New Testament?

7. Do you think it is accidental that every time the Bible lists all the Apostles, Peter is always *first* while Judas Iscariot, who betrayed Jesus, is always dead *last*? (See Matthew 10:2–5, Mark 3:16–19, Luke 6:14–17, and Acts 1:13.)

8. When we say the Pope is infallible, do we mean that he never sins? (Hint: Pope John Paul II goes to confession once a week. See footnote 22 on page 16 of *Beginning Apologetics 1*; *CCC* 890–891.)

9. Can an infallible Pope still make personal mistakes unrelated to teaching faith and morals, such as Peter's inconsistent behavior in Galatians 2:11–14?

10. Read footnote 24 on page 17 of *Beginning Apologetics 1*. How does St. Irenaeus' statement contrast with the popular opinion that one religion is as good as another? (See *CCC* 830, 834, 838.)

11. Do we Americans have a tendency to minimize authority and to rely on our independent judgement?

12. How do the lessons of the 20th century highlight the need for an unshakable rock of doctrinal stability like John Paul II? (Hint: what other world leader has stood up for the defenseless unborn, the indissolubility of marriage, and the ancient Christian teaching on contraception?)

Digging Deeper:

CCC 862, 869–870, 880–882, 891–892, 936, 2035–2037, 2039.

Jurgens 211, 381, 571, 573, 575, 580.

Scott Butler, Norman Dahlgren, and David Hess, *Jesus, Peter and the Keys: A Scriptural Handbook on the Papacy* (Queenship Publishing Company, 1997).

(Read pages 18–20)

Discussion Questions:

1. Have you ever had difficulties talking about Mary with a Protestant friend?

2. How would the fourth commandment apply to Jesus in the Holy Family? (See Exodus 20:12; *CCC* 2197–2198.) Did Jesus quit practicing this commandment after his resurrection and ascension?

3. Is the fourth commandment strictly limited to honoring parents? (See *CCC* 2199.) As Christians, should we follow the example of Jesus in honoring Mary?

4. What is the distinction between *honoring* someone and *worshipping* someone? Do your Protestant friends ever confuse these two different religious practices? Are Catholics ever allowed to worship any creature?

5. Is it biblical to refer to Our Lady as the "Blessed Virgin Mary"? (See Luke 1:26–48.)

6. Have you ever known a Protestant who realized the founders of Protestantism believed that Mary was the Mother of God and that she was Ever-Virgin? (See Appendix 2, page 20 of *Beginning Apologetics 1*.)

7. Why should Mary be called the Mother of God? Have members of your group support the answer doctrinally, with scripture, and using the early Church Fathers.

8. Is the Assumption of Mary mentioned in the Bible? Does the Bible say that everything Jesus and the Apostles did and taught is included in the Bible? (See John 21:25.)

9. Has there been a growing rigidity against honoring Mary since the beginnings of Protestantism? (See quotations from Luther, Zwingli, and Calvin on page 20 of *Beginning Apologetics 1*.)

Digging Deeper:
CCC 484–511, 721–726, 963–975, 2617–2619.

Father Frank Chacon, "Defending the Marian Dogmas" (San Juan Catholic Seminars). Item #CD–2 (2-CDs) or #CS–2 (2-cassettes).

Chacon and Burnham, *Beginning Apologetics 6: How to Explain and Defend Mary.* In clear and concise language, this booklet answers the most common questions about Mary. It also demonstrates the biblical basis for Catholic Marian beliefs and devotions (San Juan Catholic Seminars). Item #BA–6.

Steve Wood, "Mary: The World's Greatest Woman" (two audiotapes with study guide).

John Henry Newman, *Mary—The Second Eve* (booklet).

(Read pages 21–23)

Discussion Questions (discussion question numbers correspond to booklet question numbers):

1. Are Catholics allowed to "adore" or "worship" anyone or anything other than God himself? (See *CCC* 2096–2097, 2110, 2112–2114.) Is it right to honor Mary with special devotion? (See *CCC* 971.)

2. In the early Church a bishop named Nestorius refused to acknowledge Mary as the Mother of God. Did the Council of Ephesus (431 AD) proclaim him to be a hero of the faith, or a heretic? (See *CCC* 466, 495; optional: see Jurgens, Vol. 3, pages 236–238.)

3. Does Mary's unique purity and holiness originate from within herself, or is she enriched "wholly from Christ?" (See *CCC* 492.)

4. Was Jesus Mary's Savior? (See Luke 1:47.)

5. (a) What are the names of the "brothers of Jesus" mentioned in the New Testament? (See Matthew 13:55.) Are these men the sons of the Blessed Virgin Mary, or another Mary? (See *CCC* 500; Matthew 13:55, 27:56, 28:1; Mark 15:40, 47; John 19:25.)

   (b) The Bible can use the word "brother" to refer to near relatives like cousins, uncles and nephews. (See Genesis 13:8, 14:16, 29:15. *The King James Version, New American Standard, and Jerusalem Bible* [13:8 only] say "brother," while the *Revised Standard Version* and *New American Bible* say "kinsman.")

6. Have any other outstanding saints besides Mary been taken body and soul into heaven? (See Genesis 5:24, Hebrews 11:5, 2 Kings 2:11; *CCC* 966, 974.)

7. (a) Can Christian doctrine develop through the course of time? (See *CCC* 66.)

   (b) What exactly does the doctrine of the Immaculate Conception say? (See *CCC* 491.)

8. Are individual Catholics allowed to have a "take it or leave it" attitude about doctrine? (See *CCC* 88.)

9. (a) Do "private revelations" belong to the official deposit of faith? (See *CCC* 67.)

   (b) When it comes to Mary, why is it advisable to study the defined doctrines first, the Church-approved apparitions next, and the unapproved apparitions last, if at all? What might be some dangers in studying the unapproved apparitions first?

10. Does the New Testament give us any hints of Mary's important intercessory role at the very beginning of Christ's public ministry and at the very beginning of the apostolic church? (See John 2:1–11, Acts 1:14; *CCC* 965.)

11. What is the biblical basis for calling Mary "blessed"? (See Luke 1:42, 48; *CCC* 2676.)

12. What is the biblical basis for praying the "Hail Mary"? (See *CCC* 2676–2677.)

13. Can the Lord's Prayer, the Rosary, or any prayer become a vain repetition if it is done thoughtlessly, irreverently, or only mechanically? (See *CCC* 2111.) What are some scriptural examples of godly repetitive prayer?

14. What can 2 Kings 13:20–21 and Acts 19:11–12 teach us about the value of saints' relics?

(Read pages 24–26)

Discussion Questions:

CONFESSION

1. In the Old Testament, was confession of sin a private affair? (See Leviticus 5:14–26.) In John the Baptist's ministry, was confession of sin a private affair? (See Mark 1:4–5.) In the New Testament, is confession of sin only a private affair? (See James 5:16.)

2. Many Protestants interpret Jesus' words in John 20:19–23 merely as a command for the Apostles to preach the Gospel; men's sins will be forgiven or retained, depending on how they receive the Gospel. Read this passage carefully. Is this really what Jesus is saying?

3. What happens when we "bottle up" our sins and refuse to acknowledge guilt? (See Psalm 32:3–5.) Do people have a need to confess (to daytime talk show hosts, or friends, or pastors, or shrinks)? Why are some more comfortable confessing to people who can't forgive their sins rather than to a priest who can?

4. Is there any sin too great to be forgiven in the confessional? (See *CCC* 982.)

5. When was the last time you went to confession? How frequently should you go? (See *CCC* 1457–1458.)

SCANDALS IN THE CHURCH

1. Were there grievous scandals in the early Church? Identify the various scandals that afflicted Christians in:

    - Corinth (1 Corinthians 5:1–7)   _____
    - Ephesus (Acts 20:29–30)   _____
    - Pergamum (Revelation 2:14–16)   _____
    - Thyatira (Revelation 2:20–24)   _____
    - Laodicea (Revelation 3:15–17)   _____

2. Below is a list of Christ's twelve handpicked, personally-trained Apostles. Draw a line connecting the appropriate number of Apostles (in parentheses) to the scandalous behaviors in the middle:

Peter		Thomas
James	**betrayed Christ** (1) Mark 14:43–44	Matthew
John	**denied Christ** (1) Mark 14:66–72	James, son of Alphaeus
Andrew	**abandoned Christ in the garden** (12) Mark 14:50	Jude, son of James
Philip	**doubted Christ's resurrection** (1) John 20:24–25	Simon the zealot
Bartholomew		Judas Iscariot

3. If there were scandals in the early Church and scandals in the Apostolic circle, should we be surprised if there are scandals in the Church today?

4. Is sexual sin caused by celibacy, by marriage, or by human weakness in a sex-soaked culture? Is it possible to live a chaste life, either married or single? (See Matthew 19:26, Philippians 4:13, 1 Corinthians 10:13, 2 Corinthians 12:9.)

5. Was Jesus celibate? Was St. Paul celibate? (See 1 Corinthians 7:8.) According to the Bible, is celibacy a good thing? (See Matthew 19:10–12, 1 Corinthians 7:32–35; *CCC* 1618–1620.)

6. Is Christ's Church made up only of the pure, or does it contain sinners as well? (Read the parable of the wheat and the tares [Matthew 13:24–30, 36–42] and the parable of the dragnet [Matthew 13:47–50] realizing that the "kingdom" in Matthew's Gospel is the Church—Matthew 16:18–19. Also see *CCC* 827.)

Digging Deeper:
CCC 1422–1498 (confession); *CCC* 825 (scandal).
Jurgens 493, 553, 602, 637, 855a.

(Read pages 27–29)

Discussion Questions:

1. Both Protestants and Catholics are familiar with a "prayer chain," where a telephone list is used to share the needs of fellow Christians. Who is included in the Catholic prayer chain but missing in the Protestant chain?

2. Suppose your child had been in a car wreck, and was fighting for his life in the intensive care unit. Wouldn't you want to call all the holiest people you know and ask for their prayers? Why wouldn't you want to invoke the prayers of the holiest saints in heaven as well? (See *CCC* 956.)

3. Why is the communion of saints a good definition of the Church? (See *CCC* 946.)

4. Communion with our fellow Christians on earth brings us closer to Christ. Wouldn't communion with the glorified saints in heaven bring us even closer to Christ? (See *CCC* 957.)

5. Can death sever a Christian's union with Christ? (See Romans 8:38.) If a Christian is still united with Christ after death, isn't he still united with Christians who haven't died? Why is the image of Christ the Vine such a good illustration of the communion of saints?

6. Even though they've died, are the saints in heaven "dead"?
    (See Mark 12:26–27.)

7. Are Catholics permitted to engage in seances? (See *CCC* 2116.)

8. If asking fellow saints on earth to intercede for us doesn't destroy Christ's role as the one mediator, why would it be destroyed by asking glorified saints in heaven to intercede for us?

9. What are some other unique roles Christ shares with us?

10. Is heaven going to be a continuation of our finite earthly existence, or a radical elevation of our nature? (See *CCC* 1026–1027.)

11. We know that computers can make millions of calculations per second and perform multiple tasks at the same time. If man-made silicon processors are capable of sophisticated multi-tasking, why wouldn't the glorified saints in heaven receive even greater capabilities, allowing them to hear and respond to our intercessions in ways that our finite minds can't even begin to comprehend? (See 1 Corinthians 2:9. Is our conception of heaven too earthbound?)

Digging Deeper:
CCC 946–962, 2683.
Jurgens 81, 572, 852.
Patrick Madrid, *Any Friend of God's is a Friend of Mine: A Biblical and Historical Explanation of the Catholic Doctrine of the Communion of Saints* (Basilica Press, 1996). Available from Envoy Products; contact 800.553.6869 or visit their website at http://www.envoymagazine.com.

(Read pages 30–33)

Discussion Questions:

1. List some of the temporal punishments King David suffered even after his sin was forgiven (2 Samuel 12:12–13): _____
   - 2 Samuel 12:14–18   _____
   - 2 Samuel 15:12–14   _____
   - 2 Samuel 16:21–22   _____
   - 2 Samuel 19:1   _____

2. What are the three conditions for committing a mortal sin? (See *CCC* 1857–1861.)

3. Is venial sin anything to worry about? (See *CCC* 1863.)

4. Is the suffering of Purgatory the same as the punishment of the damned? (See *CCC* 1031.)

5. Is St. Paul's warning in 1 Corinthians 3:10–17 directed to Christians or non-Christians?

6. According to 1 Corinthians 3:10–17, is it possible for Christians to suffer a purifying fire?

7. Is it significant that Martin Luther, when confronted by the scriptural evidence of an intermediate state of purification (2 Maccabees 12:42–46 [NAB]; verses 42–45 [RSVCE]), decided to throw this book out of the Old Testament canon? What do Luther's actions say about the explicitness of 2 Maccabees' testimony?

8. Did Luther have the authority to remove seven books from the canon of the Bible? Does any human being?

9. Which book of the Old Testament has more references to the resurrection than the rest of the Old Testament books put together? (See 2 Maccabees 12:43; 7:9, 11, 14, 23, 29, 36; 14:46. The other Old Testament references to the resurrection are Daniel 12:2, Psalm 16:10–11, and Job 19:25–26.)

10. 2 Maccabees records the persecution of the Jews under Antiochus Epiphanes. This is a preview of the persecution of Christians under the anti-Christ. Because of their hope in the resurrection, a mother and her seven sons had the courage to face martyrdom (see 7:1–42). What might a Christian in the last days gain from their example? What might a Christian in the last days lack if we get rid of 2 Maccabees?

11. What might be some of the consequences of not praying for our beloved dead?

12. Did the early Church believe in Purgatory and recommend praying for the dead? (See Jurgens 352, 367, 382, 852, 853.)

Digging Deeper:
Steve Wood, "Purgatory" (audiotape with study guide).

(Read pages 34–36)

Discussion Questions (discussion question numbers refer to booklet question numbers):

1. How do we know that Jesus' prohibition against calling hypocrites "father" was not meant as an absolute prohibition against calling any spiritual leader, or even a parent, "father"?

2. (a) Did the Old Testament permit images that "pointed symbolically toward salvation by the incarnate Word"? (See *CCC* 2130.)

    (b) What significant event did the early Church use to justify the veneration of images and icons in the New Covenant? (See *CCC* 2131–32, 2141.)

3. Did Catholic practices, such as the Eucharistic liturgy, begin before or after the conversion of Constantine in 312 AD? (See *CCC* 1342, 1345.)

4. (a) Is the Mass a *re-presentation* of Jesus' once-for-all sacrifice, or an additional and unrelated sacrifice? (See *CCC* 1366–1367.)

    (b) What is the worldwide sacrifice among the gentile nations predicted by Malachi 1:11? (See Jurgens 8, 135, 232.) Does any other world religion (Judaism, Protestantism, Islam, Buddhism, Hinduism, and paganism) even claim to have a worldwide sacrifice?

5. (a) Is "regeneration" just a fancy way of saying "being born again"?

    (b) Why is being born of "water and spirit" mentioned in the "born again" passage in John 3:3–5? How did the early Church understand this passage? (See Jurgens 92 [and corresponding footnote 4, p. 37], 306 [and footnote 7, p. 129], 810a [and footnote 11, p. 367].)

    (c) Why do you think "born again" fundamentalist preachers so seldom refer to Titus 3:5 and John 3:5 when quoting John 3:3?

    (d) How did the early Church interpret Titus 3:5? (See Jurgens 181 [and footnote 10, p. 77], 407 [and footnote 2, p. 180].)

Digging Deeper:
Navarre Bible: The Epistle to the Hebrews, commentary on Hebrews 8:3–6 and 9:25–26.
Steve Wood, "Have You Been Born Again?" (audiotape with study guide).

(Read pages 36–37)

Discussion Questions (discussion question numbers refer to booklet question numbers):

6. (a) What reason does the *Catechism of the Catholic Church* give for baptizing infants? (See *CCC* 1250–1252.)

    (b) Did the early Church baptize infants? (See Jurgens 201, 394i, 496, 501, 585.)

    (c) Must our faith grow after baptism? (See *CCC* 1254.)

7. (a) Does any English translation of Romans 3:28 say that we are justified by faith ALONE?

    (b) What is the only verse in the New Testament that contains the words "justified," "faith," and "alone." (Read James 2:24.) What does this verse do to Luther's claim that we are justified by "faith alone"?

    (c) Do Catholics believe in salvation (justification, being made righteous) by grace? (See *CCC* 1996.)

8. (a) When "works" are mentioned in the New Testament, are they always bad? (Read Ephesians 2:8–10, Matthew 5:16, Colossians 1:10, John 10:32, Acts 9:36, 2 Timothy 3:16–17, Hebrews 10:24, James 2:26.)

    (b) What do these passages say about the necessity of "good" works?

    (c) Do Catholics believe in salvation by doing the "works of the law"? Do Catholics believe in salvation by grace, which includes the necessity of good works? (See Romans 3:28, Ephesians 2:8–9.)

9. (a) Did St. Paul presume that his salvation was so secure that he could never lose it? (See 1 Corinthians 9:27.) Did he warn the Corinthians about the possibility of losing their salvation? (See 1 Corinthians 10:1–12.) What does this do to the notion "once saved, always saved"?

    (b) What happens to a righteous man who turns to wickedness at the end of his life? (See Ezekiel 33:7–20.)

Digging Deeper:
Steve Wood, "Justification: God's Greatest Work" (two audiotapes with study guide).

(Read pages 38–39)

Discussion Questions (discussion question numbers refer to booklet question numbers):

10. Is tradition in the Bible always bad? Give two or three verses that talk about "bad" tradition. Give two or three verses that talk about "good" tradition.

11. (a) God obviously intends organic growth in nature. Does God intend a similar spiritual growth in his kingdom as well? (See Matthew 13:31–33.)

    (b) Did Jesus teach his disciples to expect growth in their understanding of his teaching? (See John 14:16, 26; John 16:12; *CCC* 91–94.)

    (c) Suppose a mother had a 21-year-old son who still looked like an infant. Would you feel sorry for her?

    (d) What would you say to a Protestant who boasted that his church is just like the Church in the book of Acts? Is this normal spiritual growth or arrested development?

12. (a) Does the Catholic Church regard celibacy as a heavy burden or a joyful witness to the kingdom of heaven? (See *CCC* 1579; Matthew 19:12.)

    (b) By praising celibacy, is the Church belittling marriage? (See *CCC* 1620.)

13. (a) How many churches did Jesus found? (See Matthew 16:18, Ephesians 4:4–6, John 10:16.)

    (b) How did St. Paul view divisions within Christ's Church? (See 1 Corinthians 1:10, Romans 16:17, Philippians 2:2.)

    (c) How did the early Church view schisms and departures from the one, true Church? (See Jurgens 1b, 48, 49, 56, 58a, 64, 257.)

14. (a) Today, where is the one and only Church founded by Jesus Christ? (See *CCC* 815–820.)

    (b) How old is Christ's Church? Did any Protestant church exist before 500 years ago? Is this an insurmountable historical problem for them?

    (c) Does the Catholic Church still teach the same doctrines—such as the Real Presence of Christ in the Eucharist, apostolic succession, and the Mass as a sacrifice—that were taught by the earliest Church Fathers? (See Jurgens 54a, 64, 128 [Eucharist]; 20, 21, 49, 65, 77, 237, 242 [apostolic succession]; 8, 21, 135, 232, 233 [sacrifice of the Mass].)

    (d) Why should we be confident that the Catholic Church will last until the end of time? (See Matthew 16:18, Matthew 28:18–20, John 14:16.)

Digging Deeper:
Steve Wood, "Early Church Fathers" (six-audiotape album designed to help you discover the writings of the early Church Fathers for yourself).

BEGINNING APOLOGETICS SERIES

All prices subject to cha
without notice.

BEGINNING APOLOGETICS 1:
**How to Explain &
Defend the Catholic Faith**
Father Frank Chacon & Jim Burnham

Gives clear, biblical answers to the most common objections Catholics get about their faith. *40 pages. (Spanish, #AE-1)*

#BA–1 $5.95

DEFENDING THE CATHOLIC FAITH
Jim Burnham
Shows you how to become an effective apologist, defend the Real Presence and the Church's incorruptibility, and discover the early Church Fathers. *4 talks, 3-CDs.*

#CD–1 $22.95

STUDY GUIDE
for Beginning Apologetics 1
Jim Burnham & Steve Wood

Guides the individual or group through 12 easy lessons. Provides discussion questions and extra material from the Bible, Catechism, and early Church Fathers. *16 pages. (#AE1-GE)*

#BA1–SG $4.95

BEGINNING APOLOGETICS 2:
**How to Answer Jehovah's
Witnesses & Mormons**
Father Frank Chacon & Jim Burnham

Targets these groups' major beliefs, and shows you how to refute them using Scripture, history, and common sense. *40 pages. (#AE-2)*

#BA–2 $5.95

BEGINNING APOLOGETICS 2.5
**Yes! You Should Believe in the Trinity:
How to Answer Jehovah's Witnesses**
Father Frank Chacon & Jim Burnham

Refutes the JWs' attack on the Trinity and provides a clear, concise theology of the Trinity. *24 pages. (#AE-2.5)*

#BA–2.5 $4.95

BEGINNING APOLOGETICS 3:
**How to Explain & Defend the Real
Presence of Christ in the Eucharist**
Father Frank Chacon & Jim Burnham

Proves the Real Presence using Scripture, early Church Fathers, and history. Gives practical ways to increase your knowledge of the Eucharist. *40 pages.*

#BA–3 $5.95

BEGINNING APOLOGETICS 4:
How to Answer Atheists & New Agers
Father Frank Chacon & Jim Burnham

Traces the roots of atheism and New Age movement. Refutes their beliefs using sound philosophy and common sense. *40 pages.*

#BA–4 $5.95

BEGINNING APOLOGETICS 5:
**How to Answer Tough
Moral Questions**
Father Frank Chacon & Jim Burnham

Answers questions about abortion, contraception, euthanasia, cloning, and sexual ethics, using clear moral principles and the authoritative teachings of the Church. *40 pages.*

#BA–5 $5.95

BEGINNING APOLOGETICS 6:
How to Explain and Defend Mary
Father Frank Chacon & Jim Burnham

Answers the most common questions about Mary. Demonstrates the biblical basis for our Marian beliefs and devotions. *40 pages.*

#BA–6 $5.95

BEGINNING APOLOGETICS 7:
**How to Read the Bible—A Catholic
Introduction to Interpreting &
Defending Sacred Scripture**
Father Frank Chacon & Jim Burnham

Provides the basic tools to read and interpret the Bible correctly. Shows how to effectively refute the errors of some modern biblical scholars. *40 pages.*

#BA–7 $5.95

BEGINNING APOLOGETICS 8:
The End Times
Father Frank Chacon & Jim Burnham

Explains what Catholics believe about the Second Coming, the Rapture, Heaven, Hell, Purgatory, and Indulgences. Refutes the errors in the "Left Behind" rapture crowd. *40 pages.*

#BA–8 $5.95

THE CATHOLIC VERSE-FINDER
Jim Burnham

Organizes over 500 verses showing the biblical basis for more than 50 Catholic doctrines—*all on one sheet of paper!* This amazing "Bible cheat sheet" helps you answer the majority of non-Catholic objections. Fold it in half, put in your Bible and never be unprepared to discuss your faith again. *1 sheet laminated, printed both sides.*

#AVF–EN $2.95

BEGINNING APOLOGETICS: BEGINNER'S DELUXE KIT
Father Frank Chacon, Jim Burnham and Steve Wood have teamed up to bring you this kit. You get …

- *Beginning Apologetics 1: How to Explain and Defend the Catholic Faith*
- Companion Study Guide
- Catholic Verse-Finder
- 12-session, CD set

**The whole set
for one price!
$44.95**

All items in the kit are available separately.

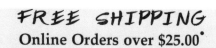